Leonardo da Vinci
1452-1519

Leonardo da Vinci (1452-1519) was born in Italy, the son of a gentleman of Florence. He made significant contributions to many different disciplines, including anatomy, botany, geology, astronomy, architecture, paleontology, and cartography.

He is one of the greatest and most influential painters of all time, creating masterpieces such as the *Mona Lisa* and *The Last Supper*. And his imagination led him to create designs for things such as an armored car, scuba gear, a parachute, a revolving bridge, and flying machines. Many of these ideas were so far ahead of their time that they weren't built until centuries later.

He is the original "Renaissance Man" whose genius extended to all five areas of today's STEAM curriculum: Science, Technology, Engineering, the Arts, and Mathematics.

You can find more information on Leonardo da Vinci in *Who Was Leonardo da Vinci?* by Roberta Edwards (Grosset & Dunlap, 2005), *Magic Tree House Fact Tracker: Leonardo da Vinci* by Mary Pope Osborne and Natalie Pope Bryce (Random House, 2009), and *Leonardo da Vinci for Kids: His Life and Ideas* by Janis Herbert (Chicago Review Press, 1998).

Little Leonardo's™

MakerLab
SPACE

Written by
BART KING

Illustrated by
GREG PAPROCKI

GIBBS SMITH
TO ENRICH AND INSPIRE HUMANKIND

To Gary Moen

Manufactured in China in January 2019 by
Crash Paper Co.

First Edition
23 22 21 20 19   5 4 3 2 1

Published by
Gibbs Smith
P.O. Box 667
Layton, Utah 84041

1.800.835.4993 orders
www.gibbs-smith.com

Designed by Sky Hatter and Renee Bond

Gibbs Smith books are printed on either
recycled, 100% post-consumer waste, FSC-
certified papers or on paper produced from
sustainable PEFC-certified forest/controlled
wood source. Learn more at www.pefc.org.

Library of Congress Control Number:
2018951288

ISBN: 978-1-4236-5115-4

INTRODUCTION

The science that deals with faraway things in the sky is called **astronomy.** You can become an astronomer in one easy step.

Want to try it? Just go outside and look up.

Now you're an astronomer. Good job!

Astronomy has to do with **outer space.** And one great thing about outer space is that there is always *more* of it to see. That's because outer space is *huge*! It's *so* huge, our minds have a hard time picturing the whole thing. But doing the activities in this book should help you imagine outer space better.

When using this book, remember:

- Read through an activity before beginning.

- Gather the supplies you'll need.

- If the activity doesn't work perfectly the first time, try again.

- Have fun.

SEEING THE SUN

To warm up your imagination, picture the Earth. Think of all the animals and people who live here. Think of how long it would take you to walk to another city. So Earth seems pretty big, right?

But a *million* Earths could fit inside our Sun.

Now *that's* big.

The Sun is also a **star,** like the ones you see in the sky. And it's not even very big compared to most of those stars. The Sun is in a category called **yellow dwarf stars.**

But big or small, the Sun is the center of our solar system. Its warmth and light keep everything on Earth alive.

CAUTION: You should *never* look directly at the Sun. (It can cook your eyeballs!)

What You Need:

⬚ Crayons or markers

What You Do:

See the picture below? Imagine that's the Sun. But is it the right color? If not, just color it in the way it should be.

Wait—are you reaching for a *yellow* crayon? If you look at the Sun from outer space (or anywhere but Earth) it's *white.* The reason the Sun looks yellow to us is because of Earth's air. (This air is called our **atmosphere.**)

But you know what? Go ahead and color it yellow. Or orange. Or red!

Because of the presence or lack of an atmosphere and the distances involved, the Sun looks different from other planets:

Mercury: Since this planet is very close to the Sun, it's twice as big in the sky on Mercury as it is on Earth.

Venus: You can barely see the Sun through this planet's thick clouds. And the sky on Venus is orange.

Mars: The Sun is farther away from Mars than Earth, so it looks smaller. The sky on Mars is butterscotch colored, and sometimes pink.

Jupiter: The clouds here are too thick to even *see* the Sun.

Saturn: The Sun is much smaller and dimmer than what we see on Earth.

Uranus and Neptune: From these two planets, the Sun looks like a very, very bright star. It's still brighter than a full Moon seen from Earth, though.

VOYAGE FROM THE SUN

The Sun is huge, but it looks pretty small from Earth. If you held up a quarter to the sky, you could cover up the whole Sun. (But don't do this, because you should *never* look at the Sun.)

In other words, the Sun looks smaller than a quarter in the sky. That's because the Sun is 93 million miles away from us. So a distance of 93 million miles is called one **astronomical unit,** or **AU.**

But how big is an AU really? Let's find out.

What You Need:

⊠ One basketball

⊠ One pea or small marble

What You Do:

1. Go outside, like in a park or big yard.

2. Set the pea down. That's Earth.

3. Now take 55 steps away from the pea. Walk in a straight line, and count the steps off as you go.

4. When you get to 55, set down your basketball. That's the Sun.

Now turn and look back at the pea. You have just made a model of two things:

- About how *big* the Earth is compared to the Sun.

- About how *far* the Earth is from the Sun. That's one AU!

What You Need to Know:

Your model is a **scale model.** That means it gives us an idea of larger sizes. In reality, you'd have to walk back 93 million miles to get to your Sun.

WHAT DO YOU THINK? In your scale model, guess how far away from the Sun that Saturn would be? What about the closest star?*

* Answers: Saturn would be about 950 feet away. And the closest star would be in Japan! (It's called Proxima Centauri.)

SUN SPOT

The Earth spins like a top. That's what makes day and night.

What You Need:

☐ One globe of the Earth (or a soccer-sized ball)

☐ One flashlight

☐ A dim or dark room

☐ A helper

What You Do:

1. Give the globe or ball to your helper.

2. Tape a little piece of paper on the globe where you live. (If you're using a ball, guess.)

3. Stand about 10 feet away. Turn on the flashlight. That's the sun. Shine the Sun at the Earth.

4. Have your helper spin the Earth slowly around. See how your home goes into the shadow? That's why we have night. When it comes around to the light again, that's morning.

5. Now trade places with your helper. Let them shine the Sun and you spin the Earth.

ORBITING EARTH

The Earth travels around the Sun in a circle. This circle is called an **orbit.** One full orbit takes one year.

What You Need:

☒ Play-Doh (if possible, orange or red, and blue or green)

☒ Optional (if no blue or green Play-Doh is available): A small blue or green ball

☒ One round pie tin (or other round cooking container)

What You Do:

1. Grab some orange or red Play-Doh.

2. Roll it into a ball.

3. Now squish that ball into the middle of the pie tin. That's the Sun.

4. Now set the blue ball in the pie tin, or roll a small blue or green Play-Doh ball and set it in the tin. That's Earth.

5. Gently roll the ball counterclockwise around the edge of the pie tin. That's the Earth's orbit.

6. How fast can you roll your Earth once around the Sun? That's one whole year in real time.

What You Need to Know:

It takes the Earth one year to orbit the Sun. But some planets have orbits that are much slower. Neptune has the slowest orbit of all the planets. Its year is equal to 164 Earth years.

ORBITING MOON

The giant rock called the Moon is our closest neighbor in space. It is the Earth's **satellite** (which is what any object that orbits a planet is called). Just as Earth orbits the Sun, the Moon orbits Earth. You can show this orbit just like before.

What You Need:

- ☒ Play-Doh (if possible, blue or green, and white)

- ☒ Optional (if no white Play-Doh is available): A small white or gray ball

- ☒ One round pie tin (or other round cooking container)

What You Do:

1. Grab some blue or green Play-Doh.

2. Roll it into a ball.

3. Squish that ball into the middle of the pie tin. That's Earth.

4. Now set the white or gray Play-Doh or ball in the pie tin. That's the Moon.

5. Gently roll the ball around the edge of the pie tin. That's the Moon's orbit.

What You Need to Know:

The Moon is a quarter the size of Earth. So it's a big satellite. We also build much smaller **artificial satellites.** We use rockets to shoot them into space. Right now there are about 1,500 of these human-made satellites orbiting the Earth.

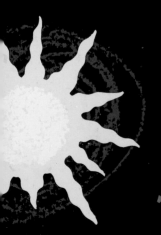

LIFT YOUR OWN WEIGHT

You are always being pulled on. The thing pulling you is called **gravity.** Gravity is a force that pulls two objects toward each other. So gravity pulls the Earth toward the Sun, and it pulls you toward the Earth. The more massive something is, the more gravity it has.

What You Need:

⊐ A bowling ball (or any object that weighs about 15 pounds)

What You Do:

1. The Moon is smaller than the Earth. So if you went to the Moon, you would weigh less than you do here. But how much less?

2. Go to a bowling alley or other place with bowling balls. Pick up a ball. (Be careful you don't drop it on your toe.)

3. That ball is pretty heavy, right? Well guess what? You just picked up yourself! On the Moon, you would weigh about as much as that bowling ball.

4. Now roll your ball down the lane. (If you get a strike, you can have a free snow cone.)

What You Need to Know:

We know the Moon orbits the Earth. That means that sometimes the Earth comes *between* the Sun and the Moon. When that happens, the Earth's shadow falls on the Moon. That shadow gives the Moon a different shape on different days.

In other words, the Earth's shadow changes what the Moon looks like to us. For example, sometimes the Moon is shaped like a banana. That's called a **crescent moon.**

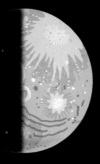

crescent   quarter   gibbous   full

Once a month, there is a **full moon.** That's when *none* of the Earth's shadow hits the Moon and we can see one whole side of it. A full moon is so bright it casts shadows on Earth. It helps us see at night.

SUPERPOWER: NIGHT VISION

When you're in bright places it's easy to see. But when it's dark, your eyes can adjust.

What You Need:

- ⋈ Your eyes
- ⋈ An outdoor spot without cars, houses, or streetlights nearby
- ⋈ A flashlight with its end covered in red cellophane

What You Do:

1. Go to your outdoor spot.

2. If you brought a light besides the red flashlight, turn it off. Wait for your eyes to adjust.

3. Look up. Have you ever wondered how many stars are in the sky? If the Moon isn't out, we can see about 3,000.

What You Need to Know:

Try not to look at regular light or you'll lose your night vision. As long as you don't look at regular light, within 30 minutes your eyes will be more than *twice* as good at seeing in the dark. It's okay to look at your flashflight though. That red covering on its end will not hurt your night vision. That's why astronomers cover their flashlights the same way.

SPOT THE SATELLITE

The International Space Station, or ISS, is an artificial satellite as big as a football field. There are always three to six astronauts living there. The ISS orbits Earth several times a day. You can see it go by if you know when to look.

What You Need:

⊠ An adult

⊠ An outdoor spot in the city or country

⊠ A smartphone with the NASA app (it's free) or one like Sky Safari (also free)

What You Do:

1. Download the free NASA app. Or go to this website with an adult and find the next scheduled flyby of the ISS in your area: https://spotthestation.nasa.gov/sightings/.

2. Find out when the ISS is going by overhead.

3. When you know what time to look and the sky is clear, go outside.

4. You don't have to wait for your eyes to adjust to the dark. The ISS is very bright.

5. Look for a big white dot moving quickly across the sky. It won't change direction or blink. That's the ISS. It's only 230 miles above you.

6. Wave hello to the astronauts!

What You Need to Know:

Imagine getting in a car and driving straight up. It would take you about an hour to leave Earth's atmosphere and hit outer space 62 miles above us.

GREENHOUSE IN THE SKY

What You Need:

☒ Binoculars

☒ Flashlight

☒ A clear evening or morning, either soon after sunset or right before sunrise

☒ An outdoor spot without cars, houses, or streetlights nearby

What You Do:

1. Look toward the horizon. Can you see what looks like a very bright silver star? If so, that's probably *not* a star. It's Venus.

2. Venus is always close to the Sun, even if the Sun isn't out yet. So if you can't spot it, look in the same direction as where the Sun is setting or rising. (But be careful not to look directly at the Sun.)

3. At night the only thing brighter than Venus is the Moon. Venus is so bright that people can even spot it during the day. And at night it can throw a shadow. See if you can spot a Venus shadow near you.

What You Need to Know:

Venus is sometimes called the Morning Star, but it's a planet about the same size as Earth. Venus has an atmosphere full of clouds. The Sun's heat gets trapped under these clouds, like a greenhouse. So Venus is the hottest planet in the solar system.

THE SPEED OF LIGHT

Did you know that light has a speed? It moves at 186,000 miles a second. That's very fast, but in space, distances are huge. When sunlight leaves the Sun, it takes 8 minutes and 20 seconds to get to us.

What You Need:

- Binoculars
- Flashlight (red cellophane optional)
- A clear night when the Moon is out
- An outdoor spot without cars, houses, or streetlights nearby

What You Do:

1. After you get to your outdoor spot, wait for your eyes to adjust to the dark.

2. Look up at the Moon. It should be bright, because the Moon is lit by the Sun. Remember, the light hitting the Moon left the Sun about 8½ minutes ago.

3. Turn on your flashlight and aim it at the Moon. Try to watch the light leave your flashlight. Can you see it start? It's hard to catch because it's so fast.

4. Your light will reach the Moon in less than 2 seconds. Turn your flashlight off after its light gets there.

5. Now look for a star. Any star. See its light? It took a long time to get to you. It takes over 4 years for light from the nearest star to get to us. And the light from other stars is much, much older.

TRY THIS: Turn on the lights in your room. The light has to leave the light bulb and then fill up the room. But this happens so fast we can't see it happen.

MOONSHOT

What You Need:

- ☒ Binoculars
- ☒ Flashlight
- ☒ A quarter
- ☒ A small orange (or another round fruit of that size)
- ☒ A clear night when the Moon is out (half moon or bigger)
- ☒ An outdoor spot without cars, houses, or streetlights nearby

What You Do:

1. When you get to your outdoor spot, wait for your eyes to adjust to the dark.

2. Look at the Moon. Compared to the Sun, the Moon is small. But from Earth, both the Sun and a full Moon look like they are the same size.

3. Hold up your quarter. Can you cover the Moon with it?

4. The Moon is slowly moving away from Earth. When the Moon was formed 4 billion years ago it was much closer than it is now.

5. Now hold up your orange—4 billion years ago, the Moon would have looked *that* big in the sky!

6. Look at the Moon through your binoculars. You can see a *lot* more detail. That same side of the Moon you see has *always* faced the Earth. That means what you're seeing is the same side of the Moon that the dinosaurs saw millions of years ago.

TRY THIS: Find a map of the Moon to bring with you the next time you go outdoors to look at the Moon. With binoculars it's easy to spot major features on the moon, like big craters. And you also should be able to easily find the Sea of Tranquility, where the first astronauts landed on the Moon.

PLANET CARDS

A **planet** is any big, round object that orbits a star—like Earth. But our Sun has other planets too. In order from nearest to farthest from the Sun, the eight planets that orbit the Sun are:

- Mercury
- Venus
- Earth
- Mars
- Jupiter
- Saturn
- Uranus
- Neptune

The Sun and its planets are the main objects that make up our **solar system.**

What You Need:

- ☐ 16 large blank index cards
- ☐ Crayons or colored markers
- ☐ A pen or pencil

What You Do:

1. Your 16 cards give you two for each planet in the solar system.

2. On one card draw a picture of Mercury. Remember, it's pretty small.

3. Do the same thing for Venus and each of the other planets. Jupiter should take up the whole card.

4. You should now have eight cards with pictures.

5. Now write the *name* of each of the planets on the other eight cards.

6. When you're done, place the cards in a stack and shuffle them.

7. Now lay the cards out on a table. How fast can you match the right picture with the right name?

GENIUS VERSION: Make extra cards for Pluto and the asteroid belt (see pages 20 and 23).

DOUBLE-GENIUS VERSION: Add fun facts about the planets on their name cards. For example:

Mercury's year lasts just 88 Earth days—but Mercury's *day* is 176 Earth days long. And even though it's closest to the Sun, Mercury has icy spots.

Venus is the third-brightest object in Earth's sky. The sun rises in the west on Venus, which is the opposite of Earth.

Earth is the only planet with liquid water on its surface.

Mars has the biggest mountain in the solar system: Olympus Mons.

Jupiter has the shortest day of any planet—nine hours and 55 minutes. But its year is 12 Earth years long.

Saturn has a ring. Also, most satellites don't have an atmosphere, but one of Saturn's satellites, Titan, has an atmosphere thicker than Earth's.

Uranus (pronounced *YUR-in-us*) is tilted on its side. So for part of the year its south pole faces the Sun, and for another part of the year its north pole does.

Neptune has winds that blow over 1,000 miles an hour.

MARS WITH THE STARS

At night some planets look like bright stars. If you're not sure if what you see is a star or a planet, use the Twinkle Rule: stars "twinkle" in the sky, but planets don't.

What You Need:

- ✴ Binoculars
- ✴ Flashlight
- ✴ A clear night in the very early morning
- ✴ An outdoor spot without cars, houses, or streetlights nearby

What You Do:

1. When you get to your outdoor spot, wait for your eyes to adjust to the dark.

2. Look for a bright star. Remember, planets don't twinkle. There are four planets you can see in the sky without a telescope: Venus, Mars, Jupiter, and Saturn. And you can always see at least *one* of them on a clear night.

3. Mars is very bright. It's not quite as bright as Venus, though. The soil on Mars has a lot of the chemical in it that creates rust. So look for a bright star with a faint red color. (If you see a bright red light in the sky that *blinks,* it's an airplane.)

4. If you have trouble finding Mars, use an astronomy app to help.

EARTH ROVER

Did you know we have a robot on Mars? The Mars Curiosity Rover is a robot as big as a car. It rolls around and collects information about the surface of Mars, and even has a laser for drilling into rocks. This rover runs on solar power. That means the Sun gives the rover the energy it needs.

What You Need:

- ▢ A wagon or wheelbarrow (you can cover the wagon in foil if you want to give it that real spaceship look)

- ▢ Some big ziplock plastic storage bags

- ▢ A cell phone to take pictures and record sounds and temperatures

- ▢ Gloves

- ▢ Imagination

What You Do:

1. Pretend you have been sent from Mars to study your neighborhood on Earth. You are in charge of an *Earth* rover. What things would Martians want to know about your neighborhood?

   - Temperature
   - Soil and rocks
   - Plants
   - Animals
   - People
   - What else?

2. Travel through your neighborhood with your rover. Collect samples in the wagon and plastic bags as you travel and use the cell phone to record your findings. Be sure to wear gloves and stay safe. Have an adult come with you if you go a long way from home.

3. Once you have enough information, write a report about what you found and what it tells you about Earth in general.

MOON MANIA

Because we call Earth's satellite the Moon, we also call other planets' satellites **moons.** Venus doesn't have a moon. Earth has one. But Jupiter has *63* moons! Some of Jupiter's moons have simple names, like Io (*EYE-oh*). Others have longer names, like Ganymede (*GAN-uh-meed*). Most of the moons in our solar system have names that come from mythology, but the names can also come from other stories.

What You Need:

⊠ Something to write with

What You Do:

1. Let's pretend that a new planet is discovered beyond Neptune. And this new planet has three moons orbiting it.

2. Come up with three good moon names to use. Be creative. You can use names of your favorite story characters—but they should sound good as a moon. For example, the two moons of Mars are named Phobos (*FOE-bos*) and Deimos (*DEE-mos*). Pretty good, right? But did you know those translate to *fear* and *terror*?

FUN FACT: Four of Jupiter's moons are so big you can see them with binoculars! And one of those moons, Ganymede, is bigger than Mercury and Pluto.

FUN FACT: An **asteroid** is a big rock that orbits the Sun. Beyond the orbit of Mars are a whole bunch of asteroids. A *really* big asteroid or satellite is called a **dwarf planet.** These are objects that aren't big enough to be planets, but are close. There are five known dwarf planets in our solar system. From biggest to smallest, they are Eris, Pluto, Haumea, Makemake, and Ceres. Even a dwarf planet can have moons (Pluto has five).

WHAT DO YOU THINK? Can moons have moons? We've never seen one, but there is no reason why not.

HOOPIN' ON SATURN

Saturn's rings are made of ice chunks. Some of the chunks are smaller than your hand and some are as big as mountains.

What You Need:

- ⌗ A hoop, like a Hula-Hoop
- ⌗ A ball (any size from a soccer ball to a beach ball will do)
- ⌗ An open area

What You Do:

1. Put the ball on the ground. That's Saturn.

2. Holding the hoop, turn around and take six steps away (because Saturn is the *sixth* planet from the Sun).

3. Turn around and face the ball.

4. Try to toss the hoop through the air so that it lands around Saturn. Your goal is to give Saturn a perfect ring.

5. You get 1 point for getting the ring around Saturn. You get 2 points if you can do it without the ring touching the planet.

BOUNCY SOLAR SYSTEM

What You Need:

- ✄ Lots of rubber bands in different colors (brown, gray, yellow, blue, green, white, red, and orange)
- ✄ Scissors
- ✄ Scratch paper
- ✄ White card stock (thin white cardboard)
- ✄ Colored markers

What You Do:

1. You're going to make planets. The center of your planets will be crumpled-up pieces of paper.

2. Tear ½ of a sheet of paper and crumple it up into a ball. Wrap gray or brown rubber bands around it. Wrap them in different directions. When you're done, this will be Mercury.

3. Crumple up 1 full sheet of paper. Around this one wrap yellow rubber bands. When you're done, that's Venus.

4. Next up is Earth. Start with 1 piece of paper and use mostly blue rubber bands. Every so often include some white and green ones too.

5. For your next planet use ⅔ of a piece of paper. Use almost all red rubber bands for Mars, with a few brown ones every so often.

6. You're using 7 sheets of paper for the next planet. Jupiter will be covered with white and orange rubber bands.

7. For Saturn, you need 5½ sheets of paper. Cover it with mostly yellow and some white rubber bands.

8. For Saturn's rings you'll use the white card stock. First, cut out a circle that will fit right around your Saturn. Once you're done, use colored markers to add colors to both

sides. Saturn's rings are pink, gray, and brown, but you can have fun and color them any way you want.

9. You need 3½ sheets of paper for Uranus. Use mostly blue rubber bands (light blue, if you have them), and a few whites and grays.

10. Use just 3 sheets of paper for the last planet, Neptune. It gets blue rubber bands.

11. Optional: You can add the dwarf planet Pluto if you want, which orbits the sun beyond Neptune. For Pluto, start with ¼ of a sheet of paper and wrap it with white rubber bands.

12. Line up your planets on the floor and turn on a flashlight at one end. That's the sun!

13. Optional: You can hang your rubber band planets as a mobile. Wrap fishing line around them and hang them up.

FUN FACT: Pluto was named by an 11-year-old girl named Venetia Burney.

COMET CHASING

A **comet** is a big chunk of ice and dirt that orbits the Sun. Sometimes those orbits go way, way out beyond the furthest planet. As the comet flies, it leaves a "tail" behind it made of bits of itself. These tails can stretch for millions of miles.

What You Need:

- Enough people to play tag
- An outdoor area

What You Do:

1. Pick one player to be the Comet.

2. The Comet tries to tag the other players.

3. If another player gets tagged, they have to follow the Comet. The tagged players are part of the Comet's tail, so they chase the Comet.

4. The last player not to get tagged wins . . . and gets to be the new Comet!

ORBIT DISTANCES

What You Need:

- [ ] A ruler or meter stick
- [ ] A pencil
- [ ] Two pieces of 8½ by 11 inch paper

What You Do:

1. Tape the two pieces of paper together to make one long rectangle 22 inches long.

2. Draw a straight line along the length of the paper that is 20 inches long.

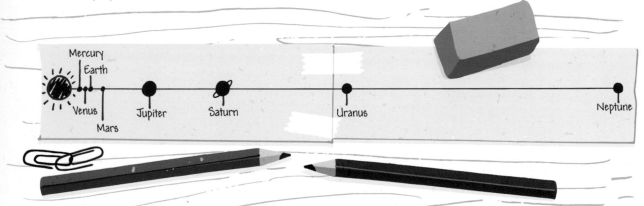

3. At the left end of that line is the Sun. Draw a large circle or curved line there to represent it.

4. Measure ¼ inch to the right of the Sun. Make a dot there. Then draw a little circle around that dot. That's Mercury.

5. At ⅜ inch from the Sun, make another dot. Draw a little circle there for Venus.

6. At ½ inch from the Sun, make a dot and draw a little circle for Earth.

7. At ¾ inch from the Sun, make a dot and draw a little circle for Mars.

8. At 2⅝ inches from the Sun, make a dot and draw a big circle for Jupiter.

9. At 5 inches from the Sun, draw a big circle with a ring for Saturn.

10. At 9 inches from the Sun, draw a medium-sized circle for Uranus.

11. At 18 inches from the Sun, draw another medium-sized circle for Neptune.

BONUS: The planets look very different when you see how far from the Sun they are. Try arranging your bouncy solar system from page 22 in this order to see how it looks.

ZERO GRAVITY

An **astronaut** is someone who travels into space. One thing astronauts have to be ready for is **zero gravity**. If you have ever been on a roller coaster you know what this feels like. You know that moment when a roller coaster finishes climbing to the top of a hill and starts going down? For those few seconds, you're weightless and experiencing zero gravity.

What You Need:

⬚ An open doorway

What You Do:

1. Stand in the doorway with your arms at your sides, palms in.

2. Reach your arms out to the sides so that the backs of your hands are pressing against the door frame.

3. Keep your elbows straight. Press the backs of your hands against the door frame as hard as you can for 30 seconds.

4. Step away from the door. Let your arms hang naturally. Your arms want to float upward, don't they? Just as if you're in zero gravity.

What You Need to Know:

Zero gravity is fun because you can float around and bounce off walls. But sometimes it makes astronauts sick. That's because the food in their stomachs is weightless too, so it's floating around and bouncing off their stomach walls.

ROCKET TO SPACE

What You Need:

☒ Balloons (different shapes are fine, but try starting with a long one)

☒ String or yarn

☒ A straw

☒ Good tape

☒ Scissors

☒ Paper

☒ Two chairs (or any other two level objects)

☒ One other person

What You Need to Know:

A **galaxy** is a group of stars and planets held together by gravity. Our galaxy is called the **Milky Way.**

What You Do:

1. Find a space in your house where you can stretch a string for a long, straight distance. It might be a hallway or across the length of your living room. Set the two chairs at each end of this length.

2. Tie one end of the string to one chair. That's the Andromeda galaxy.

3. Unroll the string all the way to the second chair. That's Earth.

4. Tape the straw to the side of a balloon (don't blow it up yet!). Then thread the string through the straw. Make sure the open end of the balloon is facing the second chair.

5. Blow up the balloon taped to the straw. Don't tie off the end of the balloon; instead, just hold it shut.

6. While you're holding the end of the balloon, have the other person tie the second end of the string to the second chair.

7. Let go of the end of the balloon. You've just launched your rocket from Earth. How far did it go? Did it reach Andromeda?

8. Try another rocket launch. This time blow up the balloon *before* taping it to the straw and threading the string through it. (You'll have to untie the string from the second chair first.)

9. Which rocket launch method worked better?

10. Cut out paper fins for your rocket. Tape them onto your balloon (*after* you blow it up). Do the fins help the rocket go farther?

11. Try more launches with different sizes of balloons. Does the size of the balloon make a difference on how far your rocket travels?

ROCKET LAUNCH

What You Need:

☐ A drinking straw

☐ Clear tape

☐ Scissors

☐ A pencil

☐ 8½ by 11 paper

☐ Colored markers or crayons

☐ A ruler

What You Need to Know:

There have only been about 540 astronauts who have flown in space. Of them, only *12* went to the Moon. And all of them went there between 1969 and 1972.

What You Do:

1. Cut a paper square that is 5 inches on each side.

2. Color one side of the square your favorite color.

3. Wrap your square tightly around the pencil with the color side out, and tape it in place.

4. Pull the pencil out of the tube of paper. The tube is now your rocket body.

5. Cut out a circle 2½ inches across. When you are done, color it on one side.

6. Cut a pie-shaped wedge from the circle. This will give the circle a mouth like Pac-Man.

7. With the color side out, bring the two straight edges of the wedge together to make a cone. Roll the paper tight so that the cone fits on top of your rocket body. When it's the right size, tape it.

8. Fit the cone on the top of your rocket body and tape it in place.

9. Cut two paper triangles about 2 inches long. These are your rocket fins. Tape them onto the rocket body at the opposite end from the cone.

10. Stick the straw in the end of your rocket with the fins. Aim it at something, like a planet. Do a mental countdown—10, 9, 8 . . . 3, 2, 1—and then *blow!*

SPACE CAPSULE

NASA launched two spaceships back in 1977: Voyager 1 and Voyager 2. The Voyager spaceships are still traveling away from Earth, and both will soon be beyond our solar system. Scientists thought there might be a possibility that they would be discovered by alien life. So each ship carries photos of our planet and sound recordings of music, birds, and whales. If aliens *do* discover the ships, they will also hear recordings of someone saying *Hello* in 56 different languages.

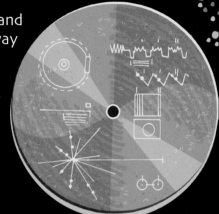

What You Need:

⊠ A box

What You Do:

1. What if *you* had to teach aliens about your life on Earth? What would you want them to know about you? Think of ideas that would help them get to know you and other humans. (Remember, we want to make a good impression!)

2. Put these items in the box or make a display of them.

3. When you think your space capsule is complete, send it off into outer space. (Or leave it somewhere where you think aliens might find it, like your brother's room.)

A CONSTELLATION OF YOU

A **telescope** is something that helps us see distant objects in outer space. Telescopes can be small enough to fit in your pocket or really big. Some of the biggest telescopes are more than 100 feet across.

The Hubble Space Telescope is as big as a school bus—and it's in space. As the Hubble orbits Earth, it sends us photos of things like planets orbiting other stars, galaxies, and constellations.

Constellations are groups of stars, like the Big Dipper. Some of their names and stories have been around for thousands of years.

Before telescopes, people would look up at the stars and imagine lines connecting one star to another to form a picture. There are 88 officially named constellations. Their names often come from Greek mythology, like Hercules, Orion, and Pegasus.

What You Need:

- ⊠ A camera
- ⊠ Someone to take your photo
- ⊠ A printer
- ⊠ Star stickers (small stars, if possible)
- ⊠ A clear plastic sheet

What You Do:

1. Have someone take your photo. It should be a full-body pose. Try doing something fun, like throwing a ball or drinking juice.

2. Print the photo on a full sheet of 8½ by 11 inch paper (larger if your printer can handle it).

3. Put a clear plastic sheet over the photo.

4. Place the star stickers around the outline of your body. That's your own personal constellation.

5. Think up names for your constellation.

6. Tape the constellation to your bedroom wall. If your star stickers glow in the dark, you'll be able to see your constellation at night.

What You Need to Know:

Stars in a constellation look like they're close to each other. But that's just how they look from Earth. They're really *trillions* of miles apart!

Every year astronomers discover new things about the universe. And you can too. Just go to a **planetarium** (*plan-uh-TARE-ee-um*). It's a big dome where they project pictures of stars and planets. It will show you how amazing and big outer space is.

WHAT DO YOU THINK? Is there a limit to outer space, or does it go on forever? Scientists don't know, but they know that it's *so* big we can't see the end of it.

GLOSSARY

ARTIFICIAL SATELLITE (ART-uh-FISH-ull SAT-uh-light): Any object made by humans that orbits a planet.

ASTEROID (AS-tur-roid): A rock that orbits the sun.

ASTRONAUT (AS-truh-not): A person who travels into space. The first astronauts were in the 1960s.

ASTRONOMY (uh-STRON-uh-me): The study of faraway things like stars, planets, and galaxies.

ASTRONOMICAL UNIT (AU) (AS-truh-NOM-ick-ull YOU-nit): The distance between the Earth and the Sun.

ATMOSPHERE (AT-muss-fear): Air that surrounds some planets and moons.

COMET (CALM-met): Small, icy objects in our solar system.

CONSTELLATION (con-stul-LAY-shun): A group of stars that seems to make the outline of an object.

CRESCENT MOON (CRESS-sent moon): The curved sliver of the Moon that we see in the sky. It will look fatter every night until it is a FULL MOON.

DWARF PLANET: Any really big asteroid or moon not quite big enough to be a planet, like Pluto.

FULL MOON: The full, round, sunlit face of the Moon that we see in the sky.

GALAXY (GAL-uck-see): A large group of stars and planets held together by gravity.

GRAVITY (GRAV-uh-tee): A force that pulls items toward each other

MILKY WAY: The name of the galaxy our solar system is a part of.

OUTER SPACE: Everything outside of Earth's atmosphere. The Moon, the solar system, and the rest of the universe are part of outer space.

ORBIT: To revolve around something.

PLANET: A large object orbiting a star. Earth is a planet orbiting the Sun.

PLANETARIUM (PLAN-uh-TARE-ee-um): A large building where stars and planets are projected on the inner surface of a giant dome.

SATELLITE (SAT-uh-light): Any object that orbits a planet. Also called a MOON.

SCALE MODEL: A small, exact copy of a larger object.

SOLAR SYSTEM (SO-lurr SIS-tum): Our Sun, and all the planets, moons, asteroids, and comets that orbit it.

STAR: A hot, massive ball of gas that's often the center of a solar system.

TELESCOPE (TELL-uh-scope): A tool to help us see far away.

YELLOW DWARF STARS: A class of fairly small stars that last about 10 billion years. The Sun is in this class.

ZERO GRAVITY (ZEER-oh GRAV-uh-tee): A condition that happens in places like outer space where the force of gravity doesn't exist. In zero gravity you feel weightless.